Durham Tales

A collection of short stories for children specially written to celebrate Durham Cathedral 900

Introduced by **Terry Deary**

Illustrated by **Linda Birch**

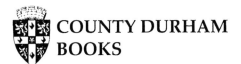

COUNTY DURHAM BOOKS

Sea Gold © Maureen Fitzsimmons, 1993
Saving the Bank © Janice Hepple, 1993
The Lost Head Hunt © Judy Powe, 1993
A Good Turn © Helen Russell, 1993
Leaving the Land © Anne English, 1993
The Poor Knight and the Giant Brawn © Vera A Hook, 1993

Illustrations © Linda Birch, 1993
Introduction © Terry Deary, 1993

Published by County Durham Books, 1993
(Durham County Council: Arts, Libraries and Museums Department)

ISBN 1 897585 05 5

CONTENTS

Introduction	*Terry Deary*	1
Sea Gold	*Maureen Fitzsimmons*	3
Saving the Bank	*Janice Hepple*	7
The Lost Head Hunt	*Judy Powe*	11
A Good Turn	*Helen Russell*	17
Leaving the Land	*Anne English*	23
The Poor Knight and the Giant Brawn	*Vera A Hook*	29

This book is dedicated to
Jenny Barnett
1950 - 1992

INTRODUCTION

Terry Deary

County Durham is the best place to live, work, bring up a family . . . and listen to stories!

But the modest northern folk haven't shared their intriguing tales and legends often enough. This is the book to put that right! All right, The Lambton Worm is known world-wide (or worm-wide) . . . but who has heard of John Duck - Durham's answer to Dick Whittington? Or the time that St Cuthbert lost his heads? And the legend of the giant brawn is far from boaring!

Writers from Somerset to Scotland entered the "Write on Durham" Competition. The best entries are published here. Local illustrator, Linda Birch, has enhanced them still further with her delightful drawings.

At last the children of Durham have a book that preserves these stories of Durham's fascinating past. 1993 was the year of Durham Cathedral's 900th birthday. *Durham Tales* is one of the enduring (and endearing) achievements of the celebrations.

Enjoy them.

SEA GOLD

Maureen Fitzsimmons

My granda tells great stories. I bet your grandad does too. But best of all is the one about Spanish treasure and Hartlepool town. Sounds unlikely, doesn't it? But it's all gospel truth, passed down from my great-granda Joe and this is how it goes.

One blustery morning in the March of 1867, Joe and his mate Davy were heading for Seaton Sands on their way to Middlesborough to look for work. Money was very scarce and jobs hard to find. Sometimes it was easier for a young lad to find work than for his father. Men had to be paid a higher wage.

There had been a tremendous storm the night before. It had rattled the windows and howled round the chimney pots of their little terraced house.

"Heaven help any ships at sea tonight," his mother had murmured as she tucked the little ones up for the night. It was hard enough to sleep with only a slice of bread and a mug of milkless tea in your stomach, without the elements throwing in their tuppence-worth!

Many a good ship had come to grief on Seaton Sands over the years. Towards the centre of the bay was a spot known as Wreck Hole. Joe had seen ships tossed up there like broken toys after a really bad gale. When Da had some cash, he and a few of the neighbours would bid for the salvage rights. Then they could have all they could rescue from the wreck. They would have to work like the clappers to strip off all the valuable timber and fittings before the next tide came in to claim the rest for old King Neptune. The rough seas could swirl the sand about and cover a wreck so that there was no trace of it left.

Joe had grown up listening to tales of a Spanish treasure ship which had run aground nearby but which had been washed out into the bay before the local men could get aboard.

"There's gold under those waves, lad. Enough gold to make us all as rich as the Queen of England! Just one snag - it's thirty fathoms or more down."

On this particular morning, the storm had caused a very odd thing to happen. As Joe and Davy trekked across the beach into the teeth of a north-easterly gale, thinking about what work they might find in the town and how the money would help at home, they suddenly realised they were walking on rock, not sand. "By, that must have been some storm last night, man! Where's all the sand gone?" "Into the Tees, I reckon," replied Davy. "Even Wreck Hole's bare! I've never heard tell of owt like this before!" Forgetting all about their errand, the lads ran down to inspect this rare sight. Bare rock pavement lay all about them with odd piles of the sea-coal which sometimes washed up from further north where the colliery workings tunnelled out under the sea. It was well worth collecting but they had a journey to make. Giddy with excitement - and hunger - Joe took a running kick at the nearest pile. It broke up into small pieces and scattered across the rocky floor of the bay. It didn't sound like coal landing. Intrigued, Joe went to investigate more closely. With a gasp, he saw gold coins, edged in black, lying at his feet. Polishing one on his coat, he gave a whoop of joy. "Davy, man, we've made us fortunes!" Davy's jaw dropped as he realised what had happened. "Fill your pockets," ordered Joe. Davy didn't need telling twice. There were still plenty of coins on the beach when they'd finished. Davy tightened his belt to stop the weight of his pockets pulling down his trousers. Looking at the mounds of coins still lying around, Joe took off his jacket and piled on as many coins as he could. Pulling the corners together he tested the weight and decided he could manage it.

"D'you reckon this is from that treasure ship the old men are always on about?" Davy asked. "Y'knaw, the Spanish dollars and gold bars that were supposed to have been on the ship that disappeared? The one the tide got to first?"

"I'd say so, wouldn't you? Just look at them. They're old for sure - and I can't rightly figure out the words on them." "Well - you don't hear a lot of Spanish round here," joked Davy, rubbing his hands together with glee. "Just think what we'll be able to get for the bairns with all this."

"I think we'd better get our dads down here quick. Old Mrs. Raine isn't going to be too keen on taking these in exchange for sugar and bacon!"

"Too true! Let's be on our way then."

So the two friends staggered back across the bay to a hearty welcome back home. The news flashed around the little community like wildfire. Parties of treasure-hunters set out with prams, pushcarts and sacks, trouping across the shore to seek their fortunes. From what Granda says quite a few did. The tide came in and put an end to their searches for a while. As soon as it turned, they were back, scrabbling and scratching . The boys, all thoughts of Middlesborough and work gone from their minds, kept a bonfire going into the night with drift-wood they found at the high-water mark. No-one wanted to leave the beach till every inch of it had been searched and the last coin safely gathered up.

"Well lads," said Joe's da that night, "you'll never do a better paid day's work than you did today. I reckon the money's heaven-sent. God knows, there's plenty of hungry mouths round here and little enough work to put bread in them. We'll see to it that no-one goes short in our street. And if there's some over, we'll share it out among the neediest in the town. But we'll keep the good news to ourselves, eh lads? No reason why the Revenue should hear of it."

Local shops put up notices saying 'Spanish dollars changed here." And as far as I know, the Revenue never did hear about the treasure-trove. Houses got painted, new furniture appeared. Some children wore new clothes for the very first time in their lives. Every family kept at least one coin for a souvenir. Great-granda invested in a small iron-monger's shop. His younger children were sent to school and did quite well for themselves. Granda took over the shop when his da died and now my da has it.

It's a strange story and sometimes - just sometimes - I wonder if it really happened. But if it didn't - where did the Spanish dollar on Granda's watch-chain come from?

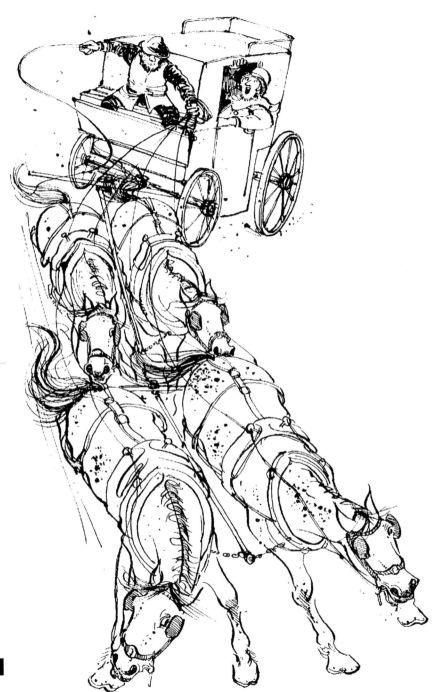

SAVING THE BANK

Janice Hepple

Money is a funny thing. Have you ever wondered how a piece of paper or sliver of metal can be worth pounds and buy you lots of things? It's all about trust. A note carries a promise that the bearer will be paid its value in gold. Not that most people would want the gold, they'd rather have what the gold could buy.

The Duke of Cleveland was a man who wanted the gold and he wanted it for rather a cruel purpose. He set out to ruin a bank by demanding gold for every note he held. The bank in question belonged to a Quaker, Jonathan Backhouse, a business rival of his.

For months the Duke had been working towards the Bank's downfall. Every time one of his tenants was due to pay the rent on his home or farm, the Duke ordered him to pay with a note from Jonathan Backhouse's bank.

Eventually he had bank notes worth a fortune. He smiled to himself when he thought of Backhouse's face when he walked into the bank and demanded gold in return for all those pieces of paper. He rubbed his hands with glee when he thought how he would point out the words, "I promise to pay..."

There wouldn't be enough gold in the whole of Darlington to pay him what he asked and what good was a bank which couldn't give its customers their gold. People would lose their trust in Backhouse's Bank and it would be ruined - just as he had planned. The Duke decided to put his plan into effect one June Saturday over a hundred years ago. But Jonathan Backhouse, sitting at his desk at the bank had learned of the devious plot to ruin his bank and decided he would not let it happen. That day was

Monday. He had until Saturday to find enough gold to pay the Duke.

Where could he get so much gold? London. But London was four days ride away. Could it be done in less? He decided he must try.

At three o'clock on Tuesday morning he set off with his servant in a coach and four. Because it was June it quickly grew light and they raced along over the dry, dusty roads, stopping only to change horses and grab a bite to eat every few hours.

Riders screamed in terror as they careered towards them and coaches pulled into hedges and rocked into ditches to get out of their way. Toll Gate coming up. "He's not stopping." shouted the gatekeeper. With a fierce hauling on the reins the horses drew up, the lead animal's nose almost touching the top bar.

"Have you got nothing smaller?" demanded the gatekeeper. "You gentry are all the same. Never carry any sensible money."

As soon as the money exchanged hands Jonathan urged the horses through the gate, leaving the gate keeper muttering behind him. There were twenty two toll gates like this to hold them up.

At midnight the travellers pulled into Grantham, a town in Lincolnshire and found a bed for the rest of the night. Half way there. It almost seemed possible that they would make the journey in time.

At the end of the second day the heavy traffic on the road told them that London was not far. Two days to reach London. Two days home.

As the doors of the Bank of England swung open for business on Thursday morning Jonathan Backhouse dashed inside, presented all the documents he needed to collect the gold and was out within minutes - bank guards following him dragging sacks of gold.

Now they carried such a heavy load, the coach which was looking rather dilapidated by now travelled more slowly. The risk of highway robbery was great.

News of their mission had reached the gatekeepers and when they heard the coach approaching they swung the gate wide to let it through without any of the hold-ups of the previous journey. Late on Friday night they reached the town of Northallerton. Not far to go, but better to arrive fresh and rested in the morning so Jonathan found lodging for the night.

Smartly dressed he set off on the last few miles of his journey, hardly daring to believe his good fortune. He planned to be seated at his desk waiting calmly when the Duke came to demand his gold.

They reached the village of Croft with plenty of time to spare when disaster struck. They came round the bend leading to the bridge, the coach swerved, the horses reared in panic and a wheel broke off its axle. The left front wheel rolled off into the reeds by the river.

Jonathan's servant would have run to the inn to get help but there was no time to repair the wheel. Acting quickly Jonathan started moving gold from the left side to the right.

Miraculously the coach balanced on its three wheels and gingerly moved off down the road.

They had half an hour to get the money to the bank. Ten minutes to opening time and the coach shuddered to a halt among the crowds who had gathered outside the Backhouse premises to see the challenge.

At ten o' clock prompt the doors opened to admit the Duke.

"Well Mr Backhouse,

I've come for my gold. I suppose you've got it," he said, supposing quite the opposite.

"Certainly Lord Darlington. It's all ready for you in my private office."

The bank clerks and customers alike smirked behind their hands as the Duke spluttered with rage

"What the ... - you hadn't it on Monday."

Jonathan's reply was to throw open the door of his office to reveal the stacks of gold inside. "Will this be enough?"

But the Duke had turned and stormed out of the bank.

THE LOST HEAD HUNT

Judy Powe

Jenny and her Mum and Dad were going to spend the Easter holiday at a friend's house near Durham Cathedral. They set out along the road to Neasham from their home near Hurworth.

"We'll take the side roads to avoid the busy A1," said Dad.

Jenny took a map and a notebook and pencil. She loved reading maps and making notes along the way.

Suddenly there was a loud BANG...

"Goodness, whatever was that?" exclaimed Mum.

"What a nuisance...we've got a puncture," said Dad, stopping the car. "I'll soon change the wheel."

They all got out of the car, and Jenny and her Mum walked along the grass verge. Mum sat down to rest on a large stone. But she sat down clumsily.

"Ow! My back! I've hurt my back!" she cried, as Dad struggled to help her to her feet and back to the car.

Now Jenny often played pretend games with imaginary people, but the little man who popped out from behind the stone seemed very real indeed. Except that he had no head. He grabbed her notebook and pencil and scribbled...

> *Hob Headless is my name*
> *To capture travellers is my game.*
> *Your Mother's back will ache and pain*
> *until you find my head again.*

Jenny was puzzled, wherever should she start looking for a lost head?

Back in the car Dad tucked a cushion behind Mum. "Perhaps we should go home" he said.

Mum smiled bravely, "It's nothing really... Please do lets go on," she persuaded him.

So they continued their journey, and soon saw the Cathedral towers in the distance.

"Grey towers of Durham, Yet well I love thy mixed and massive piles..." quoted Dad. "Sir Walter Scott wrote that. Soon, Jenny, you'll see what a powerful building it is."

They crossed the river Wear, and found their friend's house at the end of North Bailey. Jenny had a good view of the Cathedral from her bedroom window. Mum suggested that Jenny and Dad should go and visit it, while she had a rest. They agreed, and, taking a guide book with them, they entered the Cathedral and walked down the nave.

"Isn't it enormous," Jenny whispered.

"It is now, but the first church was a little wooden shrine for St Cuthbert's bones and relics." Dad explained.

"Who was St Cuthbert?" asked Jenny.

"He was Bishop of Lindisfarne in Northumberland, where he died. Two hundred years later when the Danes invaded, the monks escaped taking Cuthbert's body with them in a carved wooden coffin. For seven years they wandered until an angel told them to come here."

While he talked they had reached some steps at the end of the choir aisle, climbing up these they came to the saint's tomb behind the high altar. Nearby Jenny saw a statue of St Cuthbert holding a head in his left hand.

"Why has he taken his head off?"

Dad laughed, "It was broken off during the sixteenth century, that's St Oswald's head he carries."

What a lot of lost heads, thought Jenny. Then St Oswald winked at her.

"I lost my body," he said.

"How," asked Jenny, overcoming her surprise.

"The pagan King Penda cut me into pieces. Only my head and hand remain here with St Cuthbert. He is famous for his miracles and healing powers you know."

"Perhaps he could heal my Mum?" said Jenny and she told St Oswald all about Hob Headless.

"That wicked Hob shall be caught. Tonight we will have a Council of War," said St Oswald's head.

Jenny spent the rest of the day in a dream. At bedtime she stared out of her window wondering if St Cuthbert and St Oswald would really come. She must have fallen asleep, and thought that it must have been the shining moon that had awakened her, until she heard a tap-tapping and saw a hand beckoning to her through the window. She opened it and saw, standing in the cobbled lane, a donkey with a bearded man wearing a long woollen robe sitting on its back. In his hand the man held St Oswald's head.

"Put on your coat, Jenny," said St Oswald's head, "and come and meet St Cuthbert and his donkey, Cuddy."

Holding St Oswald's helping hand, Jenny jumped down into the lane. "Oh'" she said to St Cuthbert, "where did you find your head?"

"It always stays with my body, child," he replied. "It is my statue that lacks a head. Now let us proceed. Our good friend St Bede, the venerable scholar and historian, gave us this latin text."

"I'm afraid I can't read latin," said Jenny.

"Then I'll translate it for you," said St Cuthbert kindly. "Now have you got a map?" Jenny nodded and took it from her pocket.

While St Cuthbert read the text, Jenny worked out the clues and St Oswald's hand pointed to the way they should go...

*"Shin down a Cliffe to Burn thy Bow.
Take A177 to Coxhoe.
Fish to east and Corn to west,
there is no time to take a rest.
Through a Field of Sedge you march,
along this road see trees of Larch.
Keep your Whitts to Bishops Town.
South east of here you'll find a mound,
where now the angels guard the bones
of Norman men and castle stones."*

"I know where that is," cried Jenny, excitedly. "It's the Fairy Hill near Bishopton... But it's not an angel mound?"

"Angels... fairies... same thing," said St Cuthbert. "Now climb onto Cuddy's back behind me, and we'll be there before you can say Cuddy-Cuthbert."

Away sped Cuddy on his little twinkling hooves and in no time at all they were trotting up Fairy Hill. At the top there was a deep dark hole full of flickering lights.

"Who disturbs our peace?" boomed a strange voice.

"Only two saints and a child who seek your advice," replied St Oswald's head. "Hob Headless is up to his old tricks again."

"Then use your head to capture him," said the voice.

"Ah" St Oswald's head looked thoughtful. "Where does this Hob reside?"

"Here," said Jenny pointing to the road between Neasham and Hurworth on her map.

"No time to lose," cried St Cuthbert, and once more Cuddy whisked them away to where Hob Headless was dancing on the road in the moonlight.

"St Cuthbert, hold my head out to him," commanded St.Oswald.

Hob Headless made a grab at it with his spiny fingers.

"If you think I'm yours, then catch me" laughed St Oswald's head, and it leapt from St Cuthbert's grasp and rolled along the road, with Hob Headless running after it. Faster and faster they raced, with Cuddy galloping behind, until they reached the fairy hill. St Oswald's head bounced over the top, followed by Hob Headless but, instead of going right over, he fell down the dark hole in the middle; where the fairy-angels captured him.

"That's the end of that," said St Cuthbert.

"We still haven't found Hob's head," Jenny reminded him "and my Mum won't be better 'til we do."

"I'll ask the fairies where to look," said St Oswald's head.

"Follow these clues," the voice inside the hill told them.

> *"Take Fighting Cocks to Darlington.*
> *Pierce a Bridge to Gain a ford.*
> *Cocks like to scratch in a Barn'y'ard*
> *Startforth from here to Bowes.*
> *There up a chimney, old and grimed,*

*in disused station house you'll find
Hob's head on north Yorks land."*

"'We'll have to go to Barnard Castle and then along the old south Durham railway line to the disused Bowes station" said Jenny, reading her map.

"Off we go again," cried St Cuthbert, and, in the twinkling of a donkey's eye, they were all peering up the chimney in Bowes station house. Sure enough there was a skull, grinning down at them. St Oswald's hand threw it high and far away... all the way to Fairy Hill in County Durham. It dropped down the hole in the hill and landed between Hob Headless' shoulders.

"Home we go, Cuddy," said St Cuthbert and soon they found themselves in the lane outside Jenny's holiday house.

She thanked them, and, with St Oswald's hand helping her, climbed back into her bedroom. She turned to wave, but the cobbled lane was empty... they had all disappeared.

In the morning Jenny's Mum was delighted. "The pain has completely gone," she beamed.

"Oh, I am glad," said Jenny, giving her a hug.

"Another funny thing" said Dad. "Someone has made lots of little hoof prints all over Palace Green beside the Cathedral."

"Perhaps" said Jenny, "it could have been a Cuddy."

This story is based on historical facts in the lives of St Cuthbert and St Oswald; the skull found by soldiers at Bowes disused railway station; the Norman fort site, Fairy Hill, at Bishopton, and the legend of Hob Headless, a brownie haunting the road between Hurworth and Neasham.

A GOOD TURN

Helen Russell

To try his luck in Durham
A young man came one day
Penniless and lonely
He trudged his weary way

So this was Durham. Well, John Duck had to admit that it was very impressive to look at, but where was it's heart? Surely there must be one butcher who would take him on as an apprentice. He was tired and he was hungry. What was the matter with him? Why did no one want him to work for them? He was young, strong, and he was willing. He knew he should have been in the Butcher's Guild, but he couldn't afford it. If only someone would give him a chance to prove himself, he'd show them.

He walked slowly into Silver Street. Not much chance of a job right in the centre of Durham, but nothing ventured nothing gained.

He stopped walking when he saw a sign over a shop which read John Heslop, Master Butcher.

Here I go again, he thought.

"Can I help you?" said the man behind the counter, as he opened the door.

"I'm looking for work sir. "John replied. "Would you please take me on as an apprentice?"

John Heslop looked at the poorly dressed youth in front of him, and said kindly.

"Where are you from, lad?"

"Cleveland sir." was the reply.

There was something about the lad's manner that made John Heslop wonder if he was telling the truth. The lad could be Scottish, he thought. If he was, he wouldn't like to admit it. It was 1654 now, but it hadn't been that long ago since the Scots had been chased back over the border when they had tried to recapture Durham. Scottish or not, he thought, I need someone in the shop, and the lad couldn't be blamed for the war.

So he said, "Alright, I'll give you a chance. You can start straight away. What's your name?"

"John Duck, sir."

John Heslop smiled.

"With a name like that perhaps you should be working for a poulterer." he said. "Let's get you something to eat before you start work, or we'll have you passing out on us."

"Ann," he called out to his daughter. "Look after this young man, will you?"

> Poor John Duck
> Was down on his luck
> When he met John Heslop's daughter
> They liked each other straight away
> So he began to court her.

They were married in St Nicholas' church the next summer, and John Duck was a very happy man.

Six months later the blow fell.

"I'm sorry, John." his father-in-law said. "But I've got to let you go. The Wardens of the Company of Butchers will not allow you into the Guild, and they will fine me more than I can afford if I keep you on.

John Duck was heartbroken. He wandered down by the banks of the river in despair. He loved Durham with it's Castle and Cathedral, and it's glorious views. He felt part of it now. It was the first real home he'd ever known, and now he would have to leave it. He not only minded for himself, but his beloved wife Ann, too. She would miss her family and friends so much.

This won't do, he thought, I mustn't be downcast, something will turn up. I'll find work somewhere. I have Ann now. I won't be alone.

On the banks of the river
With his head held high
John Duck saw a raven
In the sky.

That raven seems to be following me, he thought, as he made his way across Framwellgate Bridge ready to leave Durham.

He stopped walking to see what the bird would do. It circled round him. He started walking again, and the bird continued to follow.

It's almost as though it wants me to turn round and go back, he thought. Then he told himself not to be so imaginative.

But at that moment the raven swooped right down in front of him and dropped a crown coin at his feet, and instead of flying straight off, it waited until John picked the coin up.

As soon as he had done so, the raven flew away as though it had accomplished a mission, and John had the strangest feeling that his life was planned out for him from that moment on.

As he stood by the river completely mystified, he heard,

"I'm sick to death of you two. I'd rather keep sheep or goats than cows any day, they'd be a lot less trouble."

"What's wrong?" said John.

"These cows are the most awkward pair I've ever had on my farm." was the reply.

"If they're no good to you," said John. "I'll take them off your hands. I can't pay you very much though."

He held out the crown to the farmer. There was a moment's pause, and John thought that the man was going to ask for more money, but no.

"Done." he said. "They're yours, and glad I am to be rid of them, too."

John Duck bought them before the farmer had time to change his mind. He knew it was the chance of a life time, and he grabbed it with both hands. He turned back across the bridge and lost no time in selling the cows in the market place, and a handsome profit he made, too.

From then on he was in the cattle selling business.

"He buys some of his stock from a cattle thief" said one of his rivals to a friend.

But no one could actually prove that he wasn't always honest.

> *If John Duck sometimes broke the law*
> *He never was found out*
> *His cleverness my friend has never*
> *Ever been in doubt.*

Not only was he clever, he was ambitious, too, and he became richer as the years went on. He cultivated friends in high places. This eventually brought him great power.

Because he was so powerful nobody dared to stop him from trading as a butcher any more. He was even accepted by the Wardens of the Butchers Company who had earlier been responsible for him being sacked. How he must have laughed with Ann about that.

He became richer still by lending money to poor people at a profit, and those who could not repay him were often put in prison.

Then in 1680 John Duck was given a great honour.

> *They made him Mayor of Durham*
> *For he was a powerful man*
> *And he bought a house in Silver Street*
> *Where he lived with his wife Ann.*

From then on he was a changed man. He became so well respected. that he was created baronet of Haswell on the Hill. It meant so much to him to be called Sir John of Haswell, that he said to his wife, "We shall live there, Ann, I shall buy a large estate and invest a lot of my money in coalmines."

But what pleased Ann the most was when he bought a hospital in Lumley for sick people to be cared for free of charge.

> *Yes, he went to live in Haswell*
> *To take care of the mines*
> *And from then on he lived his life*
> *On very different lines.*

> *He shared his wealth with others*
> *And gave a lot away*
> *But Haswell couldn't hold him*
> *He decided not to stay.*

After a while John went back to where he felt life had really begun for him many years earlier. To his beloved Durham. His heart had always been there, and he wasn't really happy living anywhere else.

"I shall never leave here again, Ann." he said, and he never did.

Although they had no children, they went to live in a large luxurious mansion in Silver Street until John died at the age of fifty nine.

Yet if it hadn't been for that raven who encouraged him to turn back when he was half way across Framwellgate Bridge, who knows? He might have been a poor man all his life, and we might never have heard of him.

If it wasn't for that raven
Who dropped a coin, so bold
This part of Durham's heritage
Might never have been told.

Sir John Duck we all know that you
Loved dear old Durham well
And always with affection
Your story we will tell.

LEAVING THE LAND

Anne English

Isobel Ingleby swooped down on her little sister, Anne, and swung her up into the air. "Come away. You're not meant to be waiting here." she whispered.

Anne chuckled as she fastened plump arms round Isobel's neck. "See Father," she said.

"No." Isobel was firm. "None of us can see him at the moment. He's expecting important visitors. You'll see him later, Anne. I promise."

And she carried the child away from the cool stone flagged hall to join the rest of the family in the big farmhouse kitchen.

Although the outer door was propped wide open, the kitchen was swelteringly hot. The glare and shimmer of the July heat seeped through the very walls. Haymaking was over, and the shorn fields nearest to the Great Haswell farmhouse gave off a dry, dusty smell. Isobel stifled a sneeze as she returned to her seat in the hall.

A stillness settled over the house. Before her father's illness the house was never quiet. Now, everyone spoke in whispers and the women tiptoed around on slippered feet.

Isobel yawned, then straightened her back as she tried to sit in a dignified manner on the hard wooden stool. For she had been given the task of greeting her father's friends, a rare responsibility when she had two older sisters.

From the parlour, where her father now lay, Isobel heard his hard dry cough. She longed to run to him, but Bess had told her that a woman's conversation was harmful to a sick man, and it could be true.

Bess had been with them for sixteen years. She'd arrived to take care of Mrs Ingleby when Margaret, the eldest daughter, was born. There was little she did not know about illness.

Yet there were new and unwelcome doubts in Isobel's mind. Once, she had believed everything Bess told her. Now she sometimes silently questioned her wisdom. Hadn't Bess told them that her father would recover? Yet still he lay gravely ill. What more could Isobel do?

Two days earlier she had hung her coral beads at the head of his bed to try and free him from nightmares. Daily, his four daughters picked sweet lemon balm and lavender flowers to tuck under his pillow, but the fever kept recurring. Then they heard him cry out, and he lay for hours hidden from them, the heavy curtains drawn round the bed.

Only his wife, now expecting her fifth child, knew how he hated being shut-in like that. William Ingleby was happiest in the open air, working in the Haswell fields or riding his bay mare to fields at Rainton or Moorhouse.

Despite his pain, he longed to walk his fields again, even to see the land stretching away to the Elemore skyline. He had worked so hard, and now... "Pray God." he murmured, day after day, "send me a son to inherit the land."

A door closed quietly as sixteen year old Margaret took her lively little sister out for a walk. The only other sound came from the kitchen where Bess was comforting Mrs Ingleby.

At the sound of hooves Isobel went to the door, shading her eyes against the sun. Her uncle, Richard Thursby, looking pale and concerned, slipped silently from his horse. "Take heart," he said gently, and hurried into the parlour.

Again Isobel waited before leading George Wadell of Easington and Christopher Richardson from Shotton to the parlour door. Both were soberly dressed as on a Sunday. Neither looked her in the eye.

With her task completed Isobel knew she should return to her work in the kitchen, but a longing to be near her father held her fast. The stone floor of the hall struck chill through her slippers and she shivered.

The parlour door had been left slightly open to try and catch a cooling breeze. From the room Isobel heard the crackle of stiff paper, then Uncle Richard's voice. "Come William, have your say. I will write it down, and those you have named are here to witness your will." Hearing the words,

Isobel trembled and sank to her knees. No-one made a will until death was closing in.

Her father's voice, weak and cracked with fever, began to speak the familiar, comforting phrases. "In the Name of God, Amen. In this year of our Lord, 1632 ... I, William Ingleby of Great Haswell in the County Palatine of Durham, yeoman ... "

His voice faded, then came back more strongly, "place my soul in the hands of Almighty God and commit my body to the ground."

Isobel knelt on the cold floor, unable to move, as a jumble of names and places reached her ears. She heard Margaret's name, then Elizabeth's, then her own name was spoken.

"Item ... to my third daughter Isobel, six score pounds for her portion. And my wish is that she shall have my lease of Fleming Field if she marry with the consent of her mother, and, if without consent, five score pounds."

Anne's name followed, then came a pause before her father began again. "Item ... my wife ..."

There was an interruption, a sudden noise as if the table was hastily pushed aside. The mens' voices rose.

"Help him."

"A drink William, a drink."

"Hold hard man, we're here."

Silently, Isobel rose to her feet and pushed open the door. Her father, ashen faced, the perspiration heavy on his forehead, leant forward in the bed. Two of his friends supported him, each with one arm behind his back and one in front so that he sat as if in a friendly cage. Richard Thursby wiped the sick man's face with a fresh towel. George Wadell held a beaker to his lips. No-one noticed her.

The attack passed and she withdrew as her father smiled up at the men and then lay back on his pillows.

"Come Richard, there is much to be done yet." His voice was stronger.

"My wife," he began again, "now being with child, my will is that, if it be a man," (his voice lingered on the words) "if it be a man, he shall have the lease of the Moorhouse and half a farm near Rainton when he be eighteen."

Isobel realised then, for the first time, the depth of his need for a son to inherit the land.

Through swirling thoughts she heard his voice, the instructions coming in whispers with many a pause. Then, with a gasping effort, the last words, "And I make my wife Elizabeth Ingleby sole executrix of this, my last will and testament."

There was a silence, then Uncle Richard's quiet voice. "I'll date it William. Now the witnesses will please sign." Then again, in a soft insistent voice. "William, you must sign. Feel the pen in your hand. Now make your mark. Fine man, fine. Now rest easy. All is done."

With a swirl of sound, little Anne rushed into the hall, clutching a posy of wild flowers and grasses picked on her walk. She darted past Isobel's outstretched arms and into the parlour. Reaching up to the high feather bed she presented the posy to her father.

"My little pet," he murmured, holding them tightly in hot fevered hands.

Anne raced back to her mother in the kitchen. In the hall Isobel wept.

In late November, when the fields were dark and sodden, and the trees of Elemore Wood stood etched on the skyline like a fringe of skeletons, Mrs Elizabeth Ingleby, widow of William, took to her bed. Throughout a day and a night, Bess and a woman from the village of Haswell stayed with her.

Towards noon on the second day Bess came once again to the kitchen door. She smiled. "Come, your mother is asking to see you all."

"Is all well?"

"Aye, indeed it is. Thanks be to God."

The four girls followed Bess as she shuffled across the dim hall. Outside the parlour door Bess straightened her back and stepped briskly into the room.

Margaret and Elizabeth entered immediately. Isobel paused her thoughts returning to the final day of her father's life. The girl tugged at her hand.

Mrs Ingleby lay in the big bed, the rich crimson curtains, of which she was so proud, looped back. She looked weary, her eyes were smudged blue hollows set in a pale face. A crumpled linen towel lay by her hand. Yet when she turned to her daughters, her eyes shone.

She reached out a hand, beckoning them to her. Each one knelt and kissed her.

At the far side of the bed the heavy wooden cradle swung gently on its stand, Bess bent over the swaddled bundle.

"Come and see the babe, my dears. A beauty, a real beauty," she crooned.

"Hug the baby," said Anne, setting off at speed. Laughing, Margaret and Elizabeth followed her. As Isobel rose from her knees, her mother caught her hand, smiling with special understanding. She nodded towards the cradle. "His name," she said, "is William."

The inventory and the will of William Ingleby of Great Haswell have survived since 1632 and are in Durham's University Library, Archives and Special Collections. The will names his daughters and tells that a 5th child is expected. Easington Parish registers (Durham County Records Office) show the baptism of a son, also William. The final entry in that register, dated 26 Sept.1653, is the marriage of William Ingleby of Moorhouse to Anne Midford of Pesspool (then an estate in Haswell).

THE POOR KNIGHT AND THE GIANT BRAWN

Vera A Hook

Daniel zoomed his aeroplane round the room, shaving it past his grandfather's right ear.

"Neee-ow...Neee-ow!" but Grand-dad was too deep in the newspaper to join in the game.

Just as Daniel began a high dive, intending to swoop under the newspaper and crash on his grandfather's chest, he heard, "Well, bless my soul! A wild boar's escaped in Durham".

"A what?" Daniel paused - the aeroplane held ready.

"A wild pig's running about the countryside..."

Daniel brought the plane into a controlled landing on the chair.

"Tell you what, Daniel," said Grand-dad, "I'll tell you the story of 'The Poor Knight And The Giant Boar' or brawn as they would call it in those days."

Daniel loved Grand-dad's stories so he scrunched up in the armchair beside him, still clutching his plane.

Well now, long, long ago there lived a huge, bad-tempered brawn. It lurked and spied, and smashed and crashed, and growled and squealed in the land alongside the river near Bishop Auckland.

Travellers said it was as big as a cow! Folk journeyed miles to avoid the area. Those who crept through its territory never knew when the red-eyed, hairy monster with its great yellow tusks would burst upon them, snorting and screaming with rage. Those who tried to track it down were lead round in circles by the crafty beast then it would charge out and frighten them half to death.

At last the people grew very angry and, to help them, the Bishop of Durham promised to pay a reward to anyone who could kill the animal.

There was only one challenger, Richard Pollard.

He was a poor knight but he was brave - and clever at sword play and at spear throwing. When he thought of the reward money Richard became determined to kill the monster.

He began to prepare carefully.

His neighbours heard, "Thwack! Thwack! Whew! Whew!" as he practised with his sword. They all laughed to see him creep about the farm land and leap out to attack sacks full of hay hanging from trees. Day after day he went out to track the brawn in the valley, then he sharpened his sword and spears till they shone.

As he passed, in his tough leather jerkin and leggings, he ignored the teasing of his neighbours.

"There goes the mighty brawn killer..." "He'll never do it!" "Not this side of Christmas!" "Pork chops! Pork chops!"

Richard was sure that he could prove them wrong so very early one morning, before anyone else was awake, he armed himself and set off. He carefully followed the brawn's movements.

As if it knew that it was pursued the beast headed off - crashing and smashing through bushes, splashing and plunging through ponds and streams with Richard battling to keep within sight. The spears were heavy and he sweated inside his leather clothes.

The brawn blundered on southwards.

Eventually Richard could see the massive walls of Raby Castle and then the roofs of Staindrop. His pounding heart almost failed when he thought the brawn might cross the River Tees.

Then all at once the wind changed direction.

And it smelled his scent.

The great animal stood like a stone - only the ugly wet snout twitched and quivered. It gave a terrifying snorting, growling challenge.

And charged!

It's pounding feet churned up the earth.

Richard hurled his first spear, which merely glanced off the beast's hairy back. So he fled into the cover of the woods.

The brawn's fiery eyes soon lost sight of him but its sensitive snout snorted on his trail.

Dashing through the trees, Richard swerved and backtracked trying to find a place to use his spears. Then he stopped on a path through a clearing and leaned against a great oak to get his breath.

Suddenly, there was the brawn.

It charged, grunting furiously.

Richard had no time to hurl a spear so he drew his gleaming sword. As the brawn dashed forward Richard leaped behind the oak tree and the creature's tusks scored deep into the bark. It swerved around and thrust its ugly head at him again and again while Richard hacked at it with his sword.

The brawn screamed with rage and hurled itself at its tormentor. In the terrible battle that followed the young knight was gored in the leg and was forced back against the tree. He could feel himself weakening.

When next the brawn, wounded and bloody, charged at him Richard braced the butt of his spear against the good oak and aimed the point directly at the animal's heart.

The giant brawn thundered towards its death and down it crashed, with the spear piercing its chest.

Richard stood over it in weary triumph. He could not carry the brawn back to prove his success so he drew his knife, cut out the animal's tongue and put it in his pocket. After the long chase and exhausting battle Richard lay down on a grassy bank, meaning only to rest awhile but he was soon fast asleep.

Along came a man with a horse and cart.

He approached the sleeping knight and saw the dead brawn.

"Oho!" he said. "Here's the very brawn the Bishop of Durham wants. Very well, he shall have it. And *I* shall claim the reward".

Quickly but quietly, the man hauled the brawn on to his cart and stole away to collect the reward for himself.

Poor Richard awoke and realised that some wicked person had stolen the great brawn so he travelled quickly back to Auckland Palace to demand to see the Bishop.

When he arrived there were crowds in the courtyard. "Have you heard? Great news..." "Aye, the great brawn is dead!" "You never saw the like..." The whole place buzzed with relief.

Richard Pollard was so angry at being cheated that he forgot his wounded leg and bounded up the steps.

"I want to see His Grace. I killed the brawn".

"Nonsense, young knight," said the guard pushing him back.

"I demand to see the Bishop of Durham. I have proof. And I claim the reward."

"Wait here," said the guard.

The people crowded round, arguing and pointing at the knight's torn leggings and battle-worn appearance.

Returning, the guard said, "His Grace will see you."

And Richard described to the Bishop the chase, the battle and how the brawn was stolen while he slept.

"And here's the proof I killed it!"

Taking out the brawn's tongue, Richard held it out for all to see.

"Quick! Examine the body," ordered the Bishop.

When it was found that Richard was speaking the truth the Bishop had to confess that the reward had already gone.

"Your Grace, I am but a poor knight. I was depending on the reward for my future."

"Hm..." thought the Bishop, as his stomach rumbled with hunger. (All this excitement had delayed his dinner time).

"I tell you what we'll do. I promise to give you all the land you can ride round before I finish my dinner. One of my men will go with you as witness." The Bishop settled down to enjoy a pleasant, relaxed meal at last.

But in no time at all he was interrupted by Richard's return. And the young knight was smiling broadly.

For he had ridden around the bishop's own palace and he was claiming THAT for his reward.

"Boy-oh-boy! A palace! Did he get it, Grand-dad? Did he?" asked Daniel excitedly.

"Well, no... The Bishop couldn't really give away his own palace. But he was so impressed with Richard that he gave him something even better for a young man. He gave him some of the finest land in the county of Durham... Coundon Moor, Birtley... Etherley and such, if my old memory's right. And it's *still* known as Pollard's Land today, you know!"

"Mm..." said Daniel. "Was it all true though?"

"Oh, I like to think so. Tell you what," said Grand-dad, "I've had an idea. How about you and me having a trip out on Saturday - to see a knight?"

"Great! I'd love it," said Daniel.

"If I remember right there's a carved gravestone at St. Andrew's Church in Auckland. It shows a knight in armour lying there ...with his feet resting on a brawn."

"Is he Richard Pollard?" asked Daniel, beginning to circle his plane again.

"Perhaps," Grand-dad said from behind the newspaper.

There was a long pause then Daniel said, "We could hunt for that wild boar - the one you said's escaped. Couldn't we?"

"When I get my spear sharpened, Daniel," laughed Grand-dad.

RESEARCH 'The County Books' Durham, Vol 2 by Sir Timothy Eden Pub: Robt. Hale Ltd. 1952
'Prince Bishop Country', The People, History & Folklore of Co. Durham by David A. Simpson. Pub:North Pennine Publishing. 1991